CHURCH OF THE DANDELIONS

CHURCH OF THE DANDELIONS

DANIEL A. ORTEGA

WALNUT STREET
—PUBLISHING—

ISBN: 979-8-9909790-6-2

Cover design by Dana Ortega

Back cover design by Lynn Hill

Walnut Street Publishing
1673 S Holtzclaw Ave
Chattanooga, TN 37404

Free Palestine

Spring 2024

Green strawberries prepare the way for summer,
I am pulling green threads –
Threatened by a little sun but
Otherwise so offensively safe.
I wish I could feed you strawberries.
I wish your stomach was full on fresh fruit and berries –
I wish I could give you someplace peaceful –
I wish the peaceful places were mine to give.
Or if I could blot out the thought that land
Is a thing to be given,
Much less taken away.
Sometimes I think there is nothing beautiful to say,
And I should stuff my mouth with straw.
I think we sing the same hymns
And pray the same prayers –
Different language, sure –
But I mean the same hum in our throats.
The same resonant hum in our chest.
I think we both look on winged things
And feel the same that in our hearts our lives are more misspent –
Seeing the songbird sing
And pick needles for their nests –
Preparing a good home for the young to last the season.
I think we together look on birds sparring on the fencepost,
Or clouds of gnats cavorting
And the expansive growth of trees
And know it is dignity to play,
So I think of the children.
Someday our children will
Have at least the same dignities the birds enjoy
This is what sustains me.
I don't know what sustains you,
You've reached for something so deep I hope I never know it.

The Roses are beautiful

The roses are beautiful
By the front steps you've swept clean.
The sculpted study
Of waxy limbs
And thorns
And petals unwrapping petals
Red as all imagining.

But what I mean is
I have seen
Your hands
And in your fingers
The snap of your clippers
Sharpened well.
Seen the deadheading
And the softly dropping
Finished flowers –
The purpose in your hands
Tying up branches
To the trellis.
I have seen in
Your hands
And eyes
And your straight back
All the hard, focused
Motions of care.

I know
Why curtains are sometimes drawn and the house goes dark
I know how much it takes to keep alive
I know nothing is kept alive
Unless needed
Or loved

And roses are not needed.
They are built to fall into –
To breathe in –
To allow for a moment to consume.
Roses are
An exercise in what is fragile;
They are an excess
Of red and green
And you have kept them alive –
Spared a portion from your cup
These years.

And maybe the rose is needed –
For how the motorist headed down the road is blessed for it
And is thereby made one iota less hopeless –
How the mail person escapes a moment into roses –
Setting the parcel on the clean swept steps by the roses.
From the periphery a little light comes in
From the periphery the burden is kneecapped drunk on roses
And flies and butterflies alike are diving
In front of the front door
The front door behind which none know
How much turmoil –
How many broken plates
And shattered words.
But out front you have been dignity
Coming from the door
To the bushes to the car to the door,
Beside the clean swept stairs,
And the bird feeder.
The roses are beautiful.

When the ceramic broke

i could not stop myself
from turning over
and fitting
the fragments back together
it was nice if also futile to watch the
jagged edges disappear against each other

only a hairline
betraying the hidden rupture
and my disappointment
when again they came so easily apart

Dandelions

The box says it's good for digestion
And the liver.
These dried leaves
In the paper bag,
In the plastic bag,
In the cardboard box.
These dried leaves
From Eastern Europe's meadows.
This is the way we are doing it, and
I'm worried I don't care enough.

The government
Doesn't want you to know
The whole dandelion is edible.
If it hasn't been poisoned
By lawn care,
Please eat it
Straight from the ground
On your hands and knees if you want.
Free greens never planted, watered, or cared about.

Put pressure on the word weed.
Forget the word weed.
Examine what has been called useless for its use.
Examine what has been called beautiful
At the expense of what is useful
Put pressure on what is called beautiful.

Ours is a church that keeps no scripture,
Brewing pots of bitter tea
Examining bitterness
Learning to love it.

CostCo Poem #1

I am shopping at the mall to buy shirts for springtime,
And I remember the last time I came here I was looking to buy
    you something.
It was our anniversary soon,
And even though I knew it was already over,
You had talked about how you hadn't had a new perfume
    since high school;
And I knew I was a fool for putting so much hope in a little
    bottle from France.
And I remember the kindness of the clerk who helped me pick
    a fragrance,
How nicely she asked, "Are we thinking floral, or spicy?" and
    showed me how to use the smelling sticks.

So I picked out something expensive and said
"I think she'll really like this."
And you did.

I am shopping at the mall.
Two teenage boys approach me,
And ask if there's anything I need them to pray for.
Maybe it was their single dangling earring and middle-parted
    hair,
But my first thought was the wrong answer could land me on
    a TikTok,
So I said that's very kind, but no thank you.

Afterwards I go to Costco,
To buy flavored seltzer water and the five-dollar rotisserie
    chicken.
I've had too much coffee and I'm about to dissociate.

Soon I'm having visions of a planet in a twin-star system where
   it is nearly always springtime, and the people who live there
   never build a house or dwelling but relax in the shade of old
   magnolia trees and live off the honeydew which grows wild
   there. And to occupy themselves they build abstract
   sculptures out of dried plant matter which is abundant and in
   the nighttime they get drunk on honeydew wine and burn
   their effigies, and sing songs to the impermanence of all
   things, and to their wild passions.

I also buy some potstickers.

Then I lose my car in the parking lot and an old man notices
   and makes some illiterate comment and laughs and his yellow
   eyes make him look like a dead blobfish which has been
   pulled up from the bottom of the ocean to heckle me.

But once I am home I am doing laundry and mopping the
   kitchen.
I feed my sourdough starter and smile because she is
   bubbling.
I have named her Joni.
Then I notice the sliced red grape on the kitchen counter, with
   the sunlight coming through it.
I am learning how close fulfillment is.
I am feeding my starter,
The kitchen is clean.

The redbuds got a false start

Don't try to be beautiful this spring.
You do not have to wear bells,
Smile excessively at children,
Or dance and be loud in crowded rooms.

Don't try to be beautiful this spring.
Don't buy new clothes and go to parties,
Or bring the best dish to potluck.

You do not have to be hopeful,
I saw you this morning
Before you had really awoken,
Before the gray clouds moved out
There was a color you and the sky shared
It was alright the soft talking in the car
It was alright the little miscommunications,
And finding the right tone in my voice.
We knew the day would get started when it would.

The redbuds got a false start
And they will learn like my grandmother's fig trees
Not to trust the month of March,
We coax them now for just a few warbling mouthfuls.

Maybe a good wind will come in with the cowbirds,
And you can believe it too the way the grass starts to chirp.

They've done the trimming
And the branches are lined up –
So many preparations to be made.

This time of year
Where the wind comes in heavy and long,
And clouds stretch like manta rays over the horizon,
Provisioned to soak what had been frozen.

My Heart is Like a Pigeon

The pigeons come to rest in power lines –
They are becoming cameras –
They are becoming television antennae –
They come to rest in the power lines
To feel the radio static in their feet –
To dream of airplanes –
To dream that their beautiful bodies have become a metal shell.

What awful birds those planes must seem through
Stereoscopic super-ultra-violet eyes,
To dream of airplanes because
There are no cats –
There is only the velocity,
And the powerful roar of your heart in your ears.

My heart is like a pigeon,
Gray in gray weather,
But in the right light a riot runs through it.

Cicadas

I.
I want to sing a song to
The midsummer storms,
To the lightning,
The sap of the roots and
The discontent of the dead.
I can think of no greater food
Than that dark liquor
Beneath our feet.

I want to sing a song to the red-eyed angels,
Seventeen years crawling mouth first in darkness
Taking in dark liquor.
Feeding on everything your
Grandmother never told you.

I wish I knew how it felt,
To break the earth,
And for the first time
Turn my once dark eyes to the sun.

I wish I knew how it felt
To climb green spires,
Shed the iniquity of my youth,
Flex my wings,
And take to the trees to howl.
I wish I knew how it felt
To turn the sky into a blender.
That is as close to redemption
As I can figure it.

II.
The fair has come to town.
We are playing ring toss.
We are buying the souvenir cup.
We are bumper cars.
Men with cotton candy faces –

There is something proper
To the marriage of the metallic,
Conjugal call of the cicada,
And the screams of children,
And the groan of motors tossing
Their bodies like tissue paper in
The pulsing lights and electric purple paint

In the rockets' red glare
A man stands alone eating a funnel cake –
Engulfed in his humanity,
And humanity swirls about him.
He curls over the cardboard boat like a kiss
Powdered sugar fingers.
Powdered sugar nose.

By his foot two cicadas fuck themselves gutless.
They are only two of many
Their husks are littered like black gum
Wrappers, with orange cellophane wings.
They go unburied on the asphalt,
The theater of their love and destruction.
The motors grinding, shoes thick with gum sticking,
The painted clowns, go-karts, carousels.

While above us full bedlam–
The ricochet and caterwaul.
Bouncing off each other like musket fire,

Rain upon us,
Catch on our shirts and tickle our necks.
With their sharp but ever so gentle talons as if to say
Be not afraid.
Their red eyes saying –
Be not afraid.

Here, I think
Though unredeemed
I am happy.

When I have died, sweep me up
With the gum wrappers,
I have lived,
It is over.

We shoot the target.
Knock the milk bottles down.
We are bumper cars.
Men with cotton candy faces.

There is a man standing, eating a funnel cake alone,
By his foot two cicadas fuck themselves gutless.

Here
I am happy.

pothos

the pale green of
new growth

the pot is too big and heavy
the flatpack bamboo shelf
strains, threatens to collapse

and up from it
a nest
of green upturned tear-shaped hands
erupt from the wrists
of green upturned tear-shaped hands

someone said
beauty curves
and that is true
but it is also
the unstudied tangle
the portion of chaos

Orange Smile

Joy is a fool
In an orange smile.
Joy must be stolen
In a world with car bombs
And greed making famine.
Joy is a fool at best.

But do not deplore me for
The joy I stole
From the dew
On the grass
On my feet,
From the
Whack of the wet grass.
Each drop
Scattering sun
Captured in them
The whole world
The orange smile
Being split outward again.

The dew in the grass
Hurled prisms
By my feet
Slipping me
Dancing me
Step by step
To my grave
But here now
My feet
Are picking up small black seeds
Stuck to me with rain and sap
Like pepper for my toes

Curling into the grass
The food for beetles
Who join me,
Their claws also
Tickling
And rowing the sticky air
Like men stuck in soup.
Their dew-drunk bodies crawling
Under the love and terror of birdsong
Which comes on windward
To me uncomprehending
As flutes blown by madmen
In protest to the laws of music.
In dissent to the maths of man.

The birds descend,
Racketing to racket
In defiance of falcons
And cold quiet
With the yammer of my own voice equally
Unmeaningful in meaningless summer beaten by
The fool crying in the orange sun
Whose tears made all anew this morning
The orange sun
Remade the world from wisps
For a day's journey
And whisking us back again to setting black

Whisking me the orange smile
Through days and
Laying me down to sleep where in my
Unmaking my dreams
My mind
Like yarn like
Separate threads knitted together

Collapse
To images not remembered.

The orange sun again in secret
Wets the grass
Calls the clouds
Calls the rain
To flow into the creek
And to the river
And to the sea of rested souls

These small black seeds I will carry you,
Carry you as far as I can,
That is what I am for
While I am collected enough to do it.
Joy real joy
And love real love
Are not luxury.
They are casting seeds.
They are rain.
The birds came and
I
Could not repress them
I
Could not stop them singing.

Ode to the sunset, a distraction

Ode to the sunset that brought me home late.
To the sunset that stole me away
From the next thing,
And the next thing,
In the endless string of things.

To the sky so much incarnadine
I understood for once the moths that come back every evening
To the lamp-post across the street,
I understood their bashing themselves
Again and again on the halogen bulb
In tight, pitiful orbits
Of singular adoration.

There is nothing uglier than this five-lane road,
The vape shops and billboards.
Nothing uglier except that the road runs westward.
With the sky in bloom
These gray boxes and desperate people seem redeemed –
Seem re-baptized so long as the fire strokes them,
So long as the shadows give them some movement.

Ode to the sun setting.
I could follow you to the coast and let you slip into the ocean,
But I will stop here in the parking lot of the barbeque restaurant on
the side of the ridgecut
That will never close
And with a family bearing each their own styrofoam takeaway.
We will stop and watch, and give you away to the hills

In the night the moth pursues the moon and finds herself
Tricked by white sheets,
And I at the close of the day am chasing what has never been further.

Ode to the sunset that brought me late to the house
Where the plants go unwatered,
The downstairs toilet doesn't flush,
And the ants stake ever greater claim over the kitchen counter.

Ode to the sunset unpossessed,
You have been a fine distraction.

River Stones

I think the fortune of the mountains is to be made high
But also to break,
And be made low.
The power of the waters is to make what was a mountain
Small and smooth
And broken.

In the washing river
The shallow waters cooled
My ankles on their rush to sea,
With their small hands caressing.

In the washing river
I took up a stone
Cold and hard in my hand,
Green river grass hanging
By pale red roots.
I asked the stone to speak
And the stone with a voice
Like the sound of the washing river answered,

Swallow me.
You will not die.
I will be the lump in your throat.

Command me to the sea and I'll go,
or carry me yourself in your pocket
It makes no difference,

I asked the stone to speak and he said
Have you come into this body,
Or out of it?

Have you felt your limits,
Have you felt your fingers on your ribs,
Or for the pulse in your neck,
Have you probed the soft animal in you,
Or probed the animal in another,
Probed their piercing blue and deep unknowable?

Have you seen them move in space,
With one foot so gently in front of the other?

Ask me
Should it mean anything to be anything?
That it should be like anything to be anything?
Is it chance
That bodies should curl against bodies so easy
And fingers slip between fingers?
And pure luck
That the words from the throats of these animals so softly spoken
could be so loud.
could carry a weight like the whole world?

I asked the stone to speak
And he said
There is nothing more to learn from me,
Please put me back.

So I put him back

The stone danced away,
It sailed over the water,
It rushed to sea,
I had to watch him go.

I am resilient like stone is resilient
And cold like stone is cold,

But I have never loved anything enough
To dissolve in it,
To be taken away and surrender to it,
Like the broken mountain in running water.

Ode to the Tufted Titmouse

Baeolophus bicolor

If I am reborn let me be a weightless thing of feathers
And my only expectation to address the morning
With two sweet notes, mine.

Let me live but not be defiled
By my diet
Of berries, bagel seasoning, french fries.
Let me live but not be defiled.

Let me be a powder baby blue
With a splash of saffron where the spear pierced my side.
Give me beady black eyes
And a simple song
And let me build a nest of sticks
And the loose threads of sweaters
Let me build a nest
And birth new issuance of my same song
And let that be enough.

The Poet in the Pursuit of what is Beautiful

The poet in pursuit of what is beautiful
Engages in agriculture.
A row of freshly planted turnips:
This is beautiful,
The vibrant green against fecund black soil,
The community farm, cooperation, fraternity of farmers:
These are beautiful
Wildflowers along the perimeter:
These are beautiful
The urge and urge and procreate urge of life:
That is beautiful.
A greater model of harmony may exist, but I am not aware of
       It.

But then there are the anthills.
I have loved and envied the ant.
A creature of smells,
Whose life is a roadmap of well worn paths,
Paths which cross between colonies.
Paths winding within the intricate tunnels of the home.
A gland for secreting paths, antennae for following.
An encyclopedia of data I lack the language or sense organs To
       comprehend.

The course of any lifetime
We'll meet with an anthill in disharmony.
And it is the duty of the farmer to confront.

What kills me most,
About a kicked ants' nest,
Is the way they go for the young.
They'll be taken somewhere
But there's nowhere anymore.

Just rabid chaos,
The network ruined.

That's how you know you've done them a blow.
When the blade of your shovel peels away and the glossy
      young are exposed,
The deep cool womb now in baking sunlight

Maybe they take the young down deeper.
Deeper than I can stick my shovel
And something will carry on.
Secretly I hope so, although
It was my task to prevent this.

I wouldn't call it beautiful, the hole they carved in the earth,
The mound of soil wet with their spit.
But it was complex anyway.
I wonder if complexity matters,
So much of human endeavor hinges around complexity, and
      complexifying.
So much hinges around imposing an order on raw materials

Such as
To restore a raised garden bed.
We'll grow turnips there on top of the destroyed nest
Pretty purple heirloom turnips, planted in neat rows.

Of the many ethical questions a human confronts, add to the
      list:
How many ants is a turnip worth?

But sometimes you meet in disharmony
An anthill
Where the order they've imposed,
Runs contrary to yours.

And you have to pry it up out of the ground with a shovel.
Collapse the tunnels on themselves.
We heard if you drop one scoop of anthill on another
The two colonies would fight, and extinguish both.
The ground beneath us became thick with them, on their
     madpath.
Frenzied marauders spurred by instinct in the jungle of grass
     towering
     above them.

I couldn't tell the difference between colony one and colony
     two.
It just looked like a bunch of ants.
And one little grasshopper who stumbled into the fray,
Though passed through untouched.

by Tegan Alspaugh

27

Birds Flirting

If you're not busy later,
Maybe we can
Climb with our
Enormous wings
To a sickening height,
Lock talons,
And spiral towards earth.
Maybe we could
Stare unblinking
At the churning landscape below us,
Our feet the unstable anchor,
And our breaking apart
At the final moment.
You will make that decision,
I don't plan on letting go

Mulberries

Mulberries soft as blisters
Ripe to oozing.
Mulberries heavy in the branches,
In the tree,
Beside the asphalt lot
Beside the clotted culvert stream.

Mulberries
Leap from the bough,
From their mothers nest,
Oh dear
Must have thought the mulberry
Splashing on my windscreen.
Oh dear
Said the splatter dried to red syrup
With the sunlight coming through.

Mulberries ripe to oozing
And the gore beneath the branches.
The gore and grit of seeds ground down,
Office workers and their cars in the asphalt lot
Cream a jam of berry mixed with mans-filth, sulfur tires grinding
seeds,
Raise a stink to heaven
That summons riots of finches,
Riots of starlings,
Cackle from the leaves saying:

here is the plenty of summer
here are we feasting shitting and fucking
while you under fluorescents in the air conditioning so cold you wear a
sweater in May
in our zeal we tore the fruits green and hard and sour,

we shook the tree to slake our hunger
but in May they come rolling, come peeling, come bursting like an
open heart in our throat
purple and red black and running

here feasting shitting and fucking
to make a mockery of you
to the tree pressing the chainlink
the tree buckling the asphalt
we our mad caravan to descend like death
and pick up again like gunsmoke

I climbed the tree to find
You have a kind of sweetness
Like ink I could not harvest gently.
Like ink on my fingers not soap but only time can clear away.
And the damage I've done by my eating
Pretending the part of a starling,
The damage I've done.
I wear on my lip,
On my collar.
A kind of sweetness
Over spoiled in the heat
Without much rain.
Hard seeds stuck in my teeth.
That kind of sweetness.

Cedar

His father showed him how to whittle.
They were hunting and the boy was young and impatient.
The father took up a stick of cedar, and with his knife shaved to the
purple heart wood
His father bade him the smell of the wood saying,
When God built his first temple, he built it out of cedar.

All the mad motion of form,
Take it into your heart,
Purple and strong like cedarwood
And hold it there until it is calm,
Reach into the soil, claw the loam
There is no shortage of fragrance in the damp soil,
Calling out "Be soothed,
Be untroubled by the happenings of form.
It is all my doing."

Dog. Wood.

A Dirge

It is finally really springtime.
Camp Jordan is awash in blooms of white.
Your humble poet stalks along the waterside seeking solitude, fungi.
Breathing swarms of gnats.

Amanita phalloides, death cap, stiff and white, six inches tall,
Her base is bulbous, her annulus is gaping.
Swallow her and in three days she cooks your liver.
It is said to be a passing of exquisite agony.

A baby is dressed in white, nested in white sheets in a woven basket
Below the fragrant trees.
Nested with plastic eggs.
Two women take up handfuls and baptize the baby's white bonnet
With blooms.
They coo coo for her attention, snapping photographs and laughing.
It will make a fine Easter card.

The baby squalls and lurches from her nest,
Pursuing some amphibian laying spawn in the stagnant pools.
She wants to put it in her mouth.

I think whoever dotted the city with these white blooming trees
Must have ordered them from a book
And did not inquire into their aroma.

My Grandma's Cast Iron

My cast iron was grandma's grandma's cast iron.
It is heavy, black, and smooth.
I will tell my children this cast iron is eons old.
I will tell my children our family does not not
Remember a time before this cast iron.
This cast iron will haunt my family,
They will have no choice but to drag it with them
Through the changes of the years,
They will retrieve my cast iron from
The smoldering ruins of their lives
Or my ghost will haunt them.

Cast iron is non-stick because of
Burnt oil that got stuck on.
My cast iron remembers a time when it had only
Tasted lard and woodsmoke.
My cast iron now knows the flavor of avocado oil.
My cast iron is so seasoned not even bad luck sticks to it.

My grandma cooks fried chicken.
My grandma cooks fried okra.
My grandma shops at Costco
Buys the big bag of frozen stir fry
With the sweet orange sauce and baby carrots
Her stove top is induction.
Her pan is Teflon.

She stirs the vegetables with a metal table fork and I say, "That
shit in that pan is poison. DuPont invented it and it's in all our
blood now."
And she says, "Well it ain't kill me yet and if you don't like it
you don't gotta eat none."
She peels the cellophane off the pack of chicken thighs in the

pink styrofoam tray and says "You ever smell boiled feathers and scalded skin? It would stink so bad you wouldn't even want to eat after it was so deep in your nose."

Snorkeling

Conasauga River, Oct '23

In the creekbed we discovered color.
Color which is a part of essence,
Color which is in all things,
Even the stones
And here the stones were red,
And yellow,
And white,

And we the scientists
Scratched the softer stone on the hard,
Worked until a thick paste was formed,
Wetted the pigments with river water
And painted our bodies in patterns flowing from our fingers
Madly,
Like the speech of the possessed
Not knowing what those patterns meant.
Maybe a spell of protection.
Or a spell to fortify
Or maybe only lines and scribbles to say
This is I, this is my body, I am here and you have seen me.

I wonder where else there is color lurking
Waiting to be revealed by the prying simian fingers of man
I wonder what lurks below the surface,
Like the fish which consider you, which are curious about you, too,
You deeply strange, deeply curious creature.
They kiss on your toes to see if you are food

I saw a snake in a hole that day
It was a small snake
A copperhead-
Choking a fish down head first-
Wagging the tail at me-
I think it would have bit me if its mouth wasn't full

The children who come after us
Will live in a different world,

Will learn to love in a different world,
But it will be the same world still,
The same waters which have flowed for all of time,
The same haunted masses of land which came out of the waters.

With the pigments on a stone I scratched a face,
A familiar face but not my own.
I think whoever this face belongs to has come here before.
The face of the gods who came from the heavens when the moment
Called for it,
The face of my ancestor maybe,
Or maybe it was the face of nobody.

The way the trees bend over roads as a doorway,
Searching for light,

The sound of water running
I don't know if this world was made for me,
Or if I have been formed and molded by it
Like water conforming to a crack in pavement

If I believe in truth, then I believe
All that has ever been is truth,
All that has been thought or spoken is true
The heights of music, the grandest designs,
And to the blackest sputtering of madness,
Truth in being
And I dare not turn away,
Sink deep into the waters,
Though cold and murky
Forward and through

Jason

you did not outlast
the fig trees you
dug behind
Your mother's house,

nor would you outlast
the two dogs in your front yard
who like so strong and joyful
had run the yard to dust.

And in my dumb child grief
more afraid of your sick eyes and belly
did not understand when you called me to your study, took me
through your library
and played for me
"what a wonderful world"
and "ring of fire"

you could not say
you were dying
so we sat and
listened
you put a handful of cassettes in my hands
turned over in your bed
and went to sleep

each summer we gather figs
the eye of each stem spills a single milky tear

My bones remember

My bones remember when I was a starfish,
When I was blind, speechless, and deaf,
A hungry mouth over the seafloor.
My bones remember questing long,
And growing weary,
And the satisfaction.
My God, I hope you too someday dream the starfish dream,
That you could taste the flesh of a decaying whale.
Know the hum of invertebrate life,
The dance of deconstruction.

My bones remember the first touches of rain on my skin,
The watery womb, a place I had outgrown.

My bones remember when I was a rabbit
And I beheld my beloved across a body of cool, calm water.
I believed in that reverie, that I could have
Ripped and sewed shut the pond, in order to be with her

My bones remember being chased over open plains, and that
            knife of white fear.
The clamp of teeth on my neck, and my life falling out of me,
Like a cascade of broken glass in sunlight.

My bones remember when we would go to war over a creek
            or even a muddy puddle we were so thirsty.
We would caw caw and hoopla and raise our clubs over our
            heads.

My bones remember when the gods first descended and
            opened our mouths and dropped hot coals of language down
            our throats, and we came bobbling out of the jungle
            scratching sticks together and calculating, calculating,
            calculating, dreaming up this strange Babylon.

A Hunger

I will be hungry tonight
In the sterile fashion
Of motel lights,

I would rather be like summer is
For all its violence.
How in high June vines creep hard at their perimeters
And all seems about to burst
Either into flame or to bloom.

That is what is called for –
A rupture
For a wind to blow,
And move away the hanging dust
From our hollows.

What is called for is that
The sun should roar
And no more come silent over the mountains,
Peeling off her peaches
With not a whisper
Keeping secrets.

That sweetheart
Comes like the milkman,
With her white eyes laughing
Slick with honey in her lap.
Seraphim, snake of fire.
I could not hate a mother
So I could not hate
The snake that swallowed me.

When you say it is finished,

I trust you mean the sun will eat us –
And heaven and earth both pass away.

At least it's a good time for swimming
At the edge where all in their undress are equals
You cannot keep me here
When the waters of myself
Come back from their freezing place –
Gone down to where the dragonflies hover.

It's a good time for swimming
Here I shed my skin on the rocks –
Slip into the vein –
And watch the buzzards
Wheeling overheard,
Waiting for the last lights to drop.

To the Quiltmakers

This is the pattern for newlyweds,
Interlocking rings, floral, checkered squares on blue.
It was sewn by my aunt
Given to my parents
And now to me.
This one is yellow,
It has fallen almost back to shreds
But my grandmother in ink once painted
Each state's flower, fifty squares of white,
Her flowing cursive
Again and again.

Bless the quiltmakers,
Bless all mothers and grandmothers
All the careful hands.
All that has brought homespun warmth against tyrannous cold.
Desiring not fame or dignities or even thanks,

All goodness maybe comes
From a needle pulling thread
All goodness maybe is combinatory
I don't want to forget this
Matter and energy are conserved, but
Goodness is not, beauty is not, constrained as these
Small work of my blood,
How good.

The tomato does not last.

In the wicker basket it goes molden.

In autumn, winter,
Springtime with yellow petals
And green pearls:

I crave pulpy flesh,
Purplish and knotted,
With running streaks of green and
Slightly sunburnt, overripe,
In a warm and sunny garden.

Then summer,
Comes an avalanche –
A hurricane –
Boiling off the plants red and steaming.
Left on neighbors doorsteps unannounced.
Grandmothers heaving sackfuls at children.
They collect top down
In market stalls –
On window sills –
On counters by the garlic.

Honeymoon,
When I glut on garnet and ruby
My hands and arms and chin
Run sweet and sticky.
My open mouth
Offending.

Until one day
My stomach turns sour

And my ardor dispels
Like dew in sunlight.

I have allowed what was precious
To become common.

Then,
The tomato sits in the wicker basket,
And moldens.

the light of the world

the light of the world
retreats to caves,
barefoot over stone floors,
pulls blind fish from shallow pools,
grills them in the light of day,
paired with salad of sorrel,
white man's foot,
and dandelion,
speaks no human language –
he would only gesture
fitfully
at the burning sun.

we reach no understanding.
he feeds me unsalted food
gives me water to drink
and sends me away.

The Gardener

The carrot stems are thick and woody from last year,
He bends with a back
That I hope is a little straighter
And pulls into the dusty air
Something short and knotted like a nose.
The nose is washed with rain collected in a barrel
And he chews and spits it out,
Saying
It sorta tastes like a carrot
And he laughs and says again
Only sorta.
"I've never heard of overwintering carrots," I said.
"Probably good reason for that," he said.
But who cannot admire the spirit of a man
Rediscovering the first science,
And whose tomatoes are growing like a jungle,
Seeded by the errant fruits of last year,
Springing by the squash plants with prickly leaves and stalks full of water
Nesting in them their juvenile fruits like yellow cigars not yet shed their blossoms
And the sunflowers ten feet tall
Thick as a club at the base.
Attracting to the trees the passing cardinals
Whose song is ceaseless.

My father's hands have been harder and softer
I have seen them mangled
More blood and grease than flesh
Pulling himself on his belly in dark places
Now his hands are only dirty
With good black dirt
In the weeds that are forever returning

Now they fuss over the wilting of a bean plant
Turning over and worrying the purple splotches of a pepper
Now they press themselves together
Conniving traps and barriers,
To contend with whitetails and rabbits as his only foes.
This is good work for my father's hands.

on rot

the dead log gives itself away to the
most delicate hands
which curl
which wrap around
and through
irresistible like
death and
in death all is useful
the path is laid for the angels
which follow after angels
endlessly
angels feasting on angels
a merry
train of
wedding guests
and the food they eat
which is the rot
is transmuted up
and through their translucent bodies
is made
new
carried through
the wind
away.

Untitled

There is no assailing this house
On Saturdays
When I have made my coffee and smoked my weed in a clean kitchen
And the light comes through the window right–
Bright and cold.

When I have been with friends the previous night and there's the
Faintest smell of loving company on my shirt,
Nursing a hangover

I am nevermore holy then,
Not knowing holy, not seeing it
But I can grasp it and feel it shaped like a dog's body in a dark room,
I can feel the fur of it –
Hear it breathing –
But I've never seen it,
Certainly not name or know it.

I know that lust is real,
And my better angels too
And so is joy,
And the feeling of falling,
The lurch in my stomach
And throwing my hands through the air trying to catch anything, to
Save myself,
The feeling of falling with nothing to hold onto –
Nothing arresting me but the ground –
And so harshly when I was a little boy playing and my bones
Fell down and snapped over a tree root –
The shock and nausea.

How constant is the tension in the arch of the bottoms of my feet –

The weight of my chest falling on my ankles –
The decision to use this tension in me.
But I want to know how to hold it,
The tension,
In my body and forget it –
To move with it and through it.

I am today slinging this tension like a bag over my shoulder,
Jostling it
Getting on and off of railcars –
Fidgeting
Holding close when I am crossing a person.
I am balancing myself –
I am steadying myself, always.

I resent to think there is sometimes no comfort to be found –
That there is no word that can be said,
Or a gesture offered to pull the broken scene back together.
But I think
Someday I will sit with iron in my heart.
And my words will hurl mountains into the seas.

No, I am rocky –
And I stumble –
But I am patient,
And I hope I am good
If God cares to know it.

Tegan

The window does not seem
So small and dim
Sitting on my floor with your light
Tall and green and simply laughing
Your friend who will be my friend
Telling me about the etchings of
Their body
Your dog pounding
Her paws
Her fur soft and washed
Her tail kicking up dust
My unswept floor
Her tongue
Licking the salt from my eyes

The Rooster

If not a god then a spirit,
Has blown in from I do not know where –
Who has escaped the chainlink fence of a past life
And fled,
Finding the neighborhood,
Behind the Motel 6, off the main road.
Living on that land and chicken-wit alone.

He is a glory –
A Fleetfoot sculpture of tangerine, and cream,
With a splotch of lipstick red flesh
Ran along the top of his scalp and hung from his nose.

I wish I could tell that rooster, who
Cock-a-doodle-doos outside my window
Every morning at the crack of dawn –
Every blessed morning –
For more than a year –
I wish I could tell him
That he maybe is a god,
Or seems to me a god,
Or at least is closer to god,
Than me.

I wish I could tell him how lucky he is,
Child of the Sun –
Ruled by and serving the Sun only,
Which he cannot hope to comprehend,
In the dull, empirical way I do,

To hear him hail the coming of the day –
Hailing with a heartsong uttered out his avian throat –
His song the same song –

The prayer without words passed
Into him from his father before him,
The same song.

I wish he could know how I envy him,
Scratching up a mouth full of foraged foods within my hedges –
Braving the yapping terriers
Flaunting a golden freedom,

But more than that,
I have watched him watch the sunset.
I have seen him, casually, idly, while picking through the lawn –
I have watched him witness
The vanishing of his god –
When the sky catches fire and goes dim.
He is witness to it,
He clucks softly, holds, and jogs out of view
To await the return of daylight.

The Golfer to his Beloved (a hole in the ground)

An erotic poem

I like the way they have you shaved for me,
That place around your hole
Buzzed almost bare
Only a few strokes and I am so close
To making my deposit in your sacred place.
It thrills me
To see
My white gift vanish
To hear
The soft sound of you receiving me.

Soup

Sometimes friends will make soup for friends when they are sick.
This is a work of alchemy,
So much greater than vegetables, protein, salt, and
Spicy things.

In time I'll believe
The earth brings forth good people –
Soup people,
Who load up their vehicles with Tupperware
Bringing vitamins and minerals to sick-plagued houses,
Banishing illness where they stop,
Barely a word of thanks accepted.
I could almost be annoyed at the grace
Which is shown in these soup people,
Threatening to exceed my dignity.

Alas,
In a world with friends who give soup I will go on living.
In a world with friends who give soup it would be an insult to die,
And in believing so I am well –
A bad spirit is driven out.

When I was texting
"thank you for the soup"
I made a typo
And sent "thank you for the soul"